CONTENT

DEDICATION

This book is dedicated to those left on the earth after the disappearance of many millions of people in an instant of time. May you find the answers you are looking for as you discover God's love in Jesus Christ.

ACKNOWLEDGMENTS

I want to thank my daughter, Julie Evans Albracht, for her encouragement and support in writing this book. Without her this project would not have been successful. Thank you to my son, Brenton Evans, and the team at XO Publishing for their professional and energetic support for this book.

Also, thanks to Jason Boyett for helping to edit and format the contents of this book and for his excellent perspective and input.

INTRODUCTION

Gone. They're just gone. Vanished into thin air. They've disappeared, and it seems to have happened in an instant.

Your friends. Your family members. People you knew from work or from the gym. The staff at the restaurant you frequent. The regulars at the coffee shop you go to each morning. Business leaders, politicians, and even a few celebrities and media personalities. One day they were here. The next day, in a moment, they simply … weren't.

They left behind vehicles and homes. Their businesses seem untouched. They've missed appointments. Deadlines have come and gone.

Even more dramatic events have happened. It's possible that cars have crashed because suddenly they had no drivers. Trains derailed. Airplanes—even passenger jets—have dropped out of the sky, with terrified passengers and flight crew but no trace of their pilots.

Teachers haven't shown up for class. Banks haven't opened. In some cities, no one is answering 911 calls or responding to fires or police callouts.

Without any warning, it feels like, suddenly, a huge portion of the earth's population has instantaneously ceased to exist. The world has plunged into chaos, and it began the moment so many people went missing.

But you're still here.

You're reading this.

You didn't disappear with the rest, and you're probably filled with questions: *What happened? Where did they go? Why did they disappear?*

And why am I still here?

After the mass disappearance of millions of people around the world, you want answers. So does everyone else.

This book has the answers. It won't just tell you the truth about what happened, but it will inform you what is about to happen in the very near future. Hopefully you have started reading in time to be prepared for the days that are to come.

You may have been given this book by someone long ago, and you just now remembered it, finding it tucked away on a bookshelf or deep within a closet.

You may be in the home of a missing relative or friend. You're searching for them and found this book displayed somewhere prominent, like a coffee table or shelf.

You may have found your way into a vacant home, office, apartment, or hotel room looking for supplies— or answers. You may be sheltering in a car. You may even have walked into an abandoned bookstore or church.

Regardless of the situation, you've found this book. Good. Take it with you. Consider it yours. Please read it all the way through, and when you've finished, share it with others.

Also, don't feel guilty if you have found yourself in one of those places—a home or office or vehicle—without permission. The world is very likely in turmoil right now, but the people who disappeared aren't worried about former concerns like trespassing or personal property. So, if you find supplies, use them. If you need shelter, take advantage of it. If you find food, eat it.

Take what you need. Resources may be precious right now, so use what you will and share with others who may have similar needs.

Be kind. The world seems to be falling apart, and kindness may be one of the few ways to hold onto your sense of humanity.

When you get a chance and feel safe, however, make sure to finish reading this book. Because in the next chapter you'll learn what has happened.

Where are the missing people? You're about to find out.

PART 1

WHERE DID THEY GO?

But let me reveal to you a wonderful secret. We will not all die, but we will all be transformed! It will happen in a moment, in the blink of an eye, when the last trumpet is blown. For when the trumpet sounds, those who have died will be raised to live forever. And we who are living will also be transformed.

—1 Corinthians 15:51–52 (New Living Translation)

In a moment. In the "blink of an eye." That's how it happened. You may or may not have heard the literal sound of a trumpet blast, as is mentioned in the passage above, but you definitely saw the aftermath. People in your life, neighborhood, and community—dozens—maybe hundreds or even thousands—vanished in an instant.

You may have even been in their presence when it happened. At the moment this book is being written, there's no way to know the exact timing of this event.

But it's possible the mass disappearance took place while you were in a meeting, at a store, even at home. One second they were there and the world was as it should be. The next second they were gone, and the world had been plunged into confusion.

What happened?

By the time you're reading this, you've no doubt heard plenty of speculation. Conspiracy theories spread even during the best of times, but after an event like this, they seem to be everywhere. It's all anyone can talk about.

Some people have suggested worldwide alien abduction or invasion. You've heard discussions of nanotechnology or artificial intelligence. Others believe it's the result of a brand-new disease developed in a lab. Some say it's a vaccination they got from a previous pandemic. Some say it's a new kind of warfare or terrorism.

If you are reading this book, you can safely ignore all those theories. The point of this book is not to add to that conversation but to stop it altogether.

This book will tell the truth about what happened.

It is not speculation, and it is not someone's opinion.

What you are about to read is the truth about the missing.

CAUGHT UP

Completed more than two thousand years ago, the Bible explained what was going to happen long before any of today's leaders took the world stage, and long before our society began moving toward its current reality.

In fact, there are many passages of Scripture that describe the mass disappearance. Jesus, the Son of God, spoke to His followers and disciples about it. Other spiritual teachers, like the Apostle Paul, wrote about it.

It just happened recently, but they were speaking prophetically about it centuries and centuries ago.

Since then, many more books have been written about this event. Many preachers, over the centuries, have given sermons about it.

The event that caused the disappearance of so many people has been commonly known as "The Rapture." Then people who disappeared shared many things in common, but here is the very most important thing they had in common:

All were followers of Jesus Christ.

The Rapture represented the disappearance of all the believing Christians in the world today. You will hear more about this later, but for now the most critical thing to understand is that the Rapture is mentioned in several places in the Bible. Though the event itself may have left you surprised, frightened, or confused, many of those who vanished had been anticipating the Rapture for years.

Some had been looking forward to it for most of their lives. Why? Because they believed what the Bible said about this long-anticipated moment.

There are multiple references to the Rapture in the Bible, but one text of Scripture describes it explicitly. Though written centuries ago, you will find that this passage accurately describes what the planet just experienced. These verses were written by the Apostle Paul in a letter to a group of church members—the Thessalonians—who lived in the first century, just a few decades after the death and resurrection of Jesus.

These new Christians believed the promise Jesus made that He would someday return again:

> *But I do not want you to be ignorant, brethren, concerning those who have fallen asleep, lest you sorrow as others who have no hope. For if we believe that Jesus died and rose again, even so God will bring with Him those who sleep in Jesus. For this we say to you by the word of the Lord, that we who are alive and remain until the coming of the Lord will by no means precede those who are asleep. For the Lord Himself will descend from heaven with a shout, with the voice of an archangel, and with the trumpet of God. And the dead in Christ will rise first. Then we who are alive and remain shall be caught up together with them in the clouds to meet the Lord in the air. And thus we shall always be with the Lord. Therefore comfort one another with these words.*
>
> **—1 Thessalonians 4:13–18 (New King James Version)**

This very well-known passage from the New Testament of the Bible details precisely what happened. Look at verse 17 again. It says, *"we who are alive and remain shall be caught up together with them in the clouds to meet the Lord in the air."*

Does that sound familiar to you? Does it sound like one of the rumors or theories you may have heard? You may have heard someone say they saw multiple people, in an instant, vanish into the air. Then again, this may not have happened exactly that way. The "vanishing" could have been instantaneous, meaning believers in Christ simply disappeared. They may have left a pile of clothing or jewelry behind. They may have dropped a purse or backpack or, if they were working, a piece of equipment.

Again, this book is being written before the Rapture when the exact details remained unclear. Some parts of this ancient teaching always felt mysterious to modern ears. Christians knew the Rapture was coming but did not know precisely what or how the event would happen. Nevertheless, those still alive when it happened were "caught up."

Now they know.

These humans were taken away from earth to heaven.

You might be wondering why we call this event "The Rapture," when those words are not used in the Bible passage above. This is because the New Testament was written in the ancient Greek language. The phrase "caught up" in 1 Thessalonians 4:17 above is an English translation of the Greek word *harpazo*, which meant "to snatch" or "to take away."

Several centuries after the Bible was written, one of the first prominent translations of Scripture wasn't in English—that language didn't yet exist—but in Latin. And that translation of the Bible used the Latin word *rapturo* in place of the Greek *harpazo*. That's where the term "rapture" comes from. It describes the process of Christian believers being taken away from earth to heaven.

BUSINESS AS USUAL

Another prominent Bible passage about what happened comes from Jesus Christ Himself. He spoke these words to His disciples one day when He was teaching them about the end times—the final days of humanity. He compared the last days of the modern world to the days of Noah before God sent a great flood to destroy the earth. He also compared it to the last days of Lot, a man who lived in the wicked cities of Sodom and Gomorrah. God destroyed these cities with fire for their sinfulness.

This is how Jesus described what was going to happen:

In those days, the people enjoyed banquets and parties and weddings right up to the time Noah entered his boat and the flood came and destroyed them all.
"And the world will be as it was in the days of Lot. People went about their daily business—eating and drinking, buying and selling, farming and building—until the morning Lot left Sodom. Then fire and burning sulfur

rained down from heaven and destroyed them all. Yes, it will be 'business as usual' right up to the day when the Son of Man is revealed. On that day a person out on the deck of a roof must not go down into the house to pack. A person out in the field must not return home. Remember what happened to Lot's wife! If you cling to your life, you will lose it, and if you let your life go, you will save it. That night two people will be asleep in one bed; one will be taken, the other left. Two women will be grinding flour together at the mill; one will be taken, the other left."
—Luke 17:27–35 (New Living Translation)

He says people will be going about their daily business when the Rapture happens. They will be buying and selling. They may be farming, or building houses, or simply going about their typical work day. They may be at the dentist or out for a jog. They may be enjoying a meal at a restaurant. Life will feel normal.

But abruptly, "business as usual" will end.

A construction team could be on a house installing a new roof, but some of them will be taken away.

A husband and wife might be asleep in bed, but one of them will vanish, leaving an empty, warm spot where they had been.

Two laborers might be out working on a farm. One will be caught up in the clouds and the other would be left behind.

A group of businesspeople could be sitting in a boardroom, but suddenly a handful of them will disappear from the meeting, leaving behind laptops and briefcases.

Do these scenarios sound familiar to you? This is what happened in the Rapture, though the name of the event is far less important than the event itself. If millions of people are missing from today's world, it's because Jesus is real. He's not just a made-up religious figure or a mythical character from a story written long ago.

He is alive. The Bible is true.

Though it was written centuries ago, the Bible said the Rapture would happen someday. Jesus said He would return for His followers and take them away with Him. That is exactly what He did. Every Christian believer who was alive at that instant was "caught up in the air" to meet the Lord.

They were raptured. They are no longer here—but are rejoicing in the presence of God in Heaven.

IN A MOMENT

Before reading more about who was taken, consider one more Bible passage that describes what happened. This passage was also written by the Apostle Paul in a letter to another group of Christians, a generation after Jesus was crucified and resurrected. These Christians lived in the city of Corinth. Paul addressed them as Corinthians.

This is what he wrote to them:

But let me reveal to you a wonderful secret. We will not all die, but we will all be transformed! It will happen in a moment, in the blink of an eye, when the last trumpet is blown. For when the trumpet sounds, those who have died will be raised to live forever. And we who are living will also be transformed.

—1 Corinthians 15:51–52 (New Living Translation)

Again, you will find that these words accurately describe what the planet experienced. The Rapture happened "in a moment." In the time it takes for you to blink your eye, the disappearance of so many citizens transformed the entire world.

The Rapture didn't just gather up the hundreds of millions of believers currently living at the time of the trumpet blast, but also the countless Christians who had died before this event. "For when the trumpet sounds," Paul wrote, "those who have died will be raised to live forever."

God resurrected the bodies of those who had already passed away. He reunited their spirits with their now glorified bodies. It's possible you heard rumors of unexplained activity at or near cemeteries. At the time this book was being written, it was impossible to be sure what this meant or what it looked like, but surely you know now.

You know these ancient Bible passages are accurate. You know they tell the truth about what happened in this instant of worldwide transformation. And now you have a name for it: The Rapture.

Believers were "caught up in the air" to be with Jesus. It happened "in the blink of an eye." A husband might have been taken, leaving the wife behind, or vice versa.

So don't believe any theories that offer explanations outside the Bible.

The missing were not taken away by aliens.

The missing were not magically purged by the universe.

The missing are not hiding away in a bunker somewhere. (Though, understandably, other people may have fled to bunkers or secret hiding places at this point.)

The missing have been raptured, just as the Bible predicted in the first century.

PART 2

WHO WAS TAKEN?

But to all who believed him and accepted him, he gave the right to become children of God.

—John 1:12 (New Living Translation)

You now know what happened: Jesus gathered up the millions of believers in the Rapture. They were caught up in the air and taken to be with Him. But what does it mean to be a "believer," in this instance?

If two people could have been asleep in bed and one was taken during this world-changing event, what is the significance of the one who was raptured?

The people who disappeared during the Rapture were Christians. They were followers of Jesus Christ. You have probably heard them referred to by any number of names:

Believers.

Evangelicals.

Born again.
Christ-followers.
The faithful.
The Church.

The Bible itself also uses multiple names to refers to these people. In the first verse of Ephesians, the Apostle Paul calls them "God's holy people" and "faithful followers of Jesus Christ" (Ephesians 1:1). Elsewhere, Scripture identifies them as "the church" or "the saints" or "the body of Christ."

Regardless of how you might refer to them, they all had one thing in common: They had accepted Jesus Christ as their Lord and Savior and committed to living their lives according to the teachings of the Bible.

The New Testament book of Romans, another ancient letter written by the Apostle Paul, describes the need for Jesus this way: *"For the wages of sin is death, but the free gift of God is eternal life through Christ Jesus our Lord"* (Romans 6:23, New Living Translation).

Christians are those who have accepted God's free gift of eternal life, through Jesus. All humans live under the burden of death because of our sin, but believers have come alive to Christ. They have surrendered their lives to Jesus, who promises an eternity with Him forever in heaven.

Accepting this gift is sometimes referred to as being "born again." That is one of the clearest ways to think about it, so let's look at the story in the Bible that explains this—the story about a religious man named Nicodemus who lived during the time of Jesus.

BORN AGAIN

There was a man named Nicodemus, a Jewish religious leader who was a Pharisee. After dark one evening, he came to speak with Jesus. "Rabbi," he said, "we all know that God has sent you to teach us. Your miraculous signs are evidence that God is with you." Jesus replied, "I tell you the truth, unless you are born again, you cannot see the Kingdom of God." "What do you mean?" exclaimed Nicodemus. "How can an old man go back into his mother's womb and be born again?" Jesus replied, "I assure you, no one can enter the Kingdom of God without being born of water and the Spirit. Humans can reproduce only human life, but the Holy Spirit gives birth to spiritual life. So don't be surprised when I say, 'You must be born again.' The wind blows wherever it wants. Just as you can hear the wind but can't tell where it comes from or where it is going, so you can't explain how people are born of the Spirit."

—John 3:1–8 (New Living Translation)

Some people hear the idea of being "born again" and think it sounds spooky or overly spiritual. At the least, it's an odd phrase. It may help to give it some context.

The entirety of the Bible, starting with the story of how God created the universe in the Book of Genesis, teaches that sin has divided us from God. God gave us life in the Garden of Eden, but the presence of sin—our decisions that go against God's law—has separated us from God. Though we are alive physically, we are spiritually dead because of sin. This keeps us from a relationship with God.

As a result of our sin, our minds are darkened, our emotions become corrupt, our bodies age and decay and our relationships struggle. Sin has become such a part of the human condition that we pass this sinful nature on to our children and grandchildren, from one generation to the next. Spiritual death and the natural tendency to rebel against God are inherent in all humans.

Paul describes this spiritual condition in Romans 7:14 as being "a slave to sin." We know the right thing to do, he writes, but our sinful nature makes it almost impossible for people to choose to do what's good:

> *I have discovered this principle of life—that when I want to do what is right, I inevitably do what is wrong. I love God's law with all my heart. But there is another power within me that is at war with my mind. This power makes me a slave to the sin that is still within me. Oh, what a miserable person I am! Who will free me from this life that is dominated by sin and death? Thank God! The answer is in Jesus Christ our Lord.*
>
> **—Romans 7:21–25 (New Living Translation)**

Only Jesus can free us from a life dominated by sin and death. If we are born, naturally, with a sinful nature and an unbelieving heart, then the only way to escape that sinful nature is rebirth—being "born again." This new birth is not into a human family but into the family of God. If we are not born again, we will live our lives in spiritual death and in rebellion against God.

Jesus came to save us from that reality. But when Jesus explained that to Nicodemus, and told the religious man he should be born again, Nicodemus didn't understand.

"How can these things be?" he asked.

EVERLASTING LIFE

In response to Nicodemus's question, Jesus further explained the need for salvation. That explanation ended up being one of the most famous verses in all of the Bible. You may have seen people hold up John 3:16 signs at football games. Even if you never attended church, you may have seen this verse on billboards or encountered it in the world:

> *For God so loved the world that He gave His only begotten Son, that whoever believes in Him should not perish but have everlasting life.*
> —John 3:16 (New King James Version)

Jesus came to save us by dying for us on the cross and paying for our sins. It is a debt we could never pay. Jesus lived a perfect life, and because of His perfect life, God accepted the death of His Son as the payment for the sins of mankind. This passage of the Bible says Jesus came into the world so that the world, through Him, could be saved.

By believing that Jesus is God's only Son sent into the world to pay for our sins, we can be born again of the Holy Spirit and saved from sin and hell. Accepting this gift of salvation must include a recognition of the Lordship of Jesus and the fact that He alone is the Savior of the world—and that recognition needs to come from a verbal confession:

> *If you openly declare that Jesus is Lord and believe in your heart that God raised him from the dead, you will be saved. For it is by believing in your heart that you are made right with God, and it is by openly declaring your faith that you are saved.*
> —Romans 10:9–10 (New Living Translation)

This text makes it clear that we must confess with our mouths that Jesus is Lord—we need to declare it verbally—while also believing in our hearts that He was raised from the dead. These are two crucial issues to understand in becoming a true believer in Christ.

For one thing, without acknowledging the Lordship of Christ, we are simply buying "fire insurance" to save us from hell and to make us feel better. But the purpose of salvation isn't just to avoid hell. We are saved so we can have a personal, loving relationship with Jesus for all of eternity.

But Jesus is holy, and we are sinful. Only when we seek His forgiveness and acknowledge Christ as Lord will He forgive us and transform the rebellion of our hearts. His forgiveness allows us to be in relationship with Him. A simple profession of faith—"okay, I believe"—that doesn't acknowledge Christ as Lord doesn't change the fundamental rebellion between us and God.

At the same time, believing that God raised Jesus from the dead is essential because it signifies that only Jesus, and no other so-called savior, guru, or religious leader, satisfied the requirements of God to save us from our sins. The resurrection of Jesus represents God's public and eternal validation that Jesus is who He said He is, and that God accepted His sacrifice for our sins. Jesus did the hard part for us that we could have never done.

Salvation occurs when we both believe and confess in accordance with God's will. That is literally all we have to do, and every living person who took those steps of belief and confession before the Rapture are now enjoying the eternal benefits of that decision. They were "caught up in the air" by the Lord and that is what happened when they suddenly disappeared. They freely received salvation from God, and they are now in the presence of the Lord.

A FREE GIFT

The Apostle Paul described salvation as a free gift. We can't earn it. We don't deserve it. We can only accept it or reject it.

Once you were dead because of your disobedience and your many sins. You used to live in sin, just like the rest of the world... But God is so rich in mercy, and he loved us so much, that even though we were dead because of our sins, he gave us life when he raised Christ from the dead. (It is only by God's grace that you have been saved!) For he raised us from the dead along with Christ and seated us with him in the heavenly realms because we are united with Christ Jesus. So God can point to us in all future ages as examples of the incredible wealth of his grace and kindness toward us, as shown in all he has done for us who are united with Christ Jesus. God saved you by his grace when you believed. And you can't take credit for this; it is a gift from God. Salvation is not a reward for the good things we have done, so none of us can boast about it. For we are God's masterpiece. He has created us anew in Christ Jesus, so we can do the good things he planned for us long ago.

—Ephesians 2:1–10 (New Living Translation)

"He has created us anew in Christ Jesus" is a phrase very similar to "born again." It means that, by accepting the gift of salvation, we are new people. We have radically transformed the purpose and direction of our lives.

Being saved and born again doesn't just mean that we now believe something we didn't believe before. You may have lived all of your life as an atheist before the Rapture. Now that you know better—now that the truth of the Rapture has convinced you of the existence of God and the salvation offered through Jesus Christ—you may be ready to reevaluate what you once believed.

But salvation and a commitment to God aren't just mental exercises. They require more than changing your mind. What you think doesn't make you a Christian. Salvation takes place when you make a radical decision to renew the purpose of your life. No longer are you living for yourself. No longer are you giving in to your sinful, rebellious nature or your human desires. You are ready to surrender your life to Christ and follow Him as your Lord.

BUT IS IT TOO LATE FOR ME?

It's not too late! The Rapture has already happened, but you still need a Savior—perhaps now more than ever. God has given everyone a free will. That means you still have the choice of making Jesus your Lord and Savior, even in a world filled with chaos and spiritual confusion. When you do, He'll bless you and help you live a life with Him in your heart giving you the love and direction you need. He'll give you the strength to endure the dark days that you are experiencing now and the even more severe time that is coming.

But without Jesus, you're on your own. You'll go through the rest of your life lost and confused and anxious about the future. Our prideful and sinful natures can keep us from enjoying the blessings God has for us. But when we humble ourselves before God and repent of our sins, He forgives us. God is loving and wants the best for us. When we fail—and as imperfect people, we definitely make mistakes from time to time—all we have to do is admit our sins and ask for His forgiveness and His merciful grace will erase the sin forever.

When we confess Jesus as our Lord and invite Him into our hearts, He renews our spirits, forgives us of all our sins and gives us the gift of eternal life. We are now capable of spiritual relationship and communion with God.

The Christian faith isn't some dead religion of rules and regulations. It is a dynamic, personal relationship with God.

Giving your life to God by confessing your sins and inviting Jesus into your life will radically change your perspective. It is the most important thing you will ever do—not just in this life right now on earth, but for all of eternity. The day you receive Christ and become born again is your spiritual birthday and the most important day in your life.

It is also why this book exists. The importance of this decision is the reason someone kept this book and left it, hoping that someone like you might find it after the Rapture. Whether they knew you or not, a believer in Jesus understood you would have questions. They recognized you would be confused. They knew you would need instructions about how to navigate the world after the faithful disappeared.

A PRAYER OF SALVATION

Are you ready to make Jesus your Lord? If so, you can be born again by praying this prayer. These words aren't magic. There is no special formula when it comes to receiving the gift of salvation. But if these words represent your heart and your beliefs, God will honor your confession. You will be eternally changed, and your salvation will be eternally secure in Jesus Christ. If you are ready, pray this prayer aloud to the Lord:

"Lord Jesus, I have sinned and rebelled against You, a holy God, and there is no excuse. I confess my sins to You now and repent of my rebellion. I ask for Your forgiveness, as I believe that You died for my sins on the cross. I receive Your forgiveness now and believe that Your blood is more powerful than my worst sins. I am now totally forgiven by You, and I forgive myself. The past is behind me. I confess You now as my Lord and Savior. I step down from the throne of my heart, and I pray that You will now sit on that throne as my Lord and King. Come into my heart and give me the gift of eternal life. I know I don't deserve it, but I receive it by faith as a free gift and now believe I am forgiven, born again, and on my way to heaven. I will live the rest of my life for You. Fill me with Your Holy Spirit and lead me, speak to me, and give me the power to make right decisions and live for You. In Jesus' name, amen."

Did you pray that prayer? If so, then congratulations! You are born again. You have just been given the promise of eternal life.

You may feel strong feelings right now or no feelings at all. For some, salvation represents a dramatic, emotional moment. Others may feel differently. Honestly, how you feel doesn't matter. Regardless of our emotions, God is faithful to His word, and you can always put your faith in Him, because He is faithful!

PART 3

WHAT DOES IT MEAN TO BE A CHRISTIAN?

For this reason we also, since the day we heard it, do not cease to pray for you, and to ask that you may be filled with the knowledge of His will in all wisdom and spiritual understanding; that you may walk worthy of the Lord, fully pleasing Him, being fruitful in every good work and increasing in the knowledge of God…

—Colossians 1:9–10 (New King James Version)

Now that you understand that the world's Christians were "taken up" in the Rapture and you know how important it is to give your heart to Jesus, you may be thinking about other people in your life—family, friends, work colleagues, and others—who claimed to be followers of Jesus.

You may be wondering if those people are still around.

Or you may not have to wonder, because you know for a fact that they were not Raptured. They are still here, and this is something that has been incredibly distressing to them. They are devastated.

You may also know some people who are indeed missing, and this surprises you. *They* were caught up in the air? These folks didn't exactly strike you as "the faithful." You're pretty sure they weren't even churchgoers.

The truth is that those who gave their lives to Christ never became perfect. They simply realized they needed God. Instead of trying to live life according to their own rules, they let God guide them and their decision-making.

Now that you have given your life to Christ, what should you do next?

"FOLLOW ME"

As a new believer, you should try to find a Bible if you don't have access to one already. We have tried to fill this little book with appropriate passages from the Bible, but "reading" the Bible through this book is like experiencing the Rocky Mountains through a photograph. Scripture is most powerful when you fully immerse yourself in it. The Bible is God's Word, and though it was written many centuries ago, God speaks to us through it.

No doubt the Rapture has resulted in many of the world's Bibles being left behind in homes, empty churches, or certain businesses. You may also find Bibles in hotels, thanks to the Gideons organization. In fact, because you are holding this book, it is very likely that there is also a Bible somewhere nearby. Go look for one.

If you find a Bible, take it with you. Don't feel guilty about taking one for yourself. Any person who owned a Bible before being raptured would absolutely want you to have it today. Keep it and read it for yourself.

When you first open the Bible, you may be confused about where to start. After all, it is a very dense book with a lot of words. With most books, you'll start at the beginning—and the beginning of the Bible starts with God's creation of the heavens and the earth—but given the current state of the world you may want to begin reading in another part of Scripture.

The best place to start is in the last half of the Bible, in the New Testament, because that tells the story of Jesus Christ. The first four books—Matthew, Mark, Luke, and John—are all about the life of Jesus and tell of His teachings. One of the clearest of these is The Gospel of John. It is a fantastic place to start reading.

There are other parts of the Bible worth reading as well. Many of those passages are quoted in this book you are reading now. You might also want to read sections from the Psalms and Proverbs, located near the middle of the Bible. These books are enlightening, filled with wisdom and very comforting.

You may also want to examine the Book of Revelation, which is the last book in the Bible. It is about the last days and describes many of the things happening now and the terrible events that are to come. Be forewarned: While the Psalms may be comforting, Revelation is not always comfortable reading. But it is important to understand in these times.

We will talk more about the importance of reading the Bible in the next chapter.

But as you read the Gospel of John in the New Testament, you'll find many uses of the word "follow." When Jesus taught His disciples and others, He gave them a command: *Follow Me.* Do what I do.

Parts of this verse of Scripture may sound familiar to you:

> *Then Jesus spoke to them again, saying, "I am the light of the world. He who follows Me shall not walk in darkness, but have the light of life."*
>
> **—John 8:12 (New King James Version)**

In following the example set by Jesus and examining His life, we see several activities that become important steps in the life of a new believer. One of them is water baptism.

BAPTISM

After the resurrection, in one of the last times the disciples saw Jesus, He gave them a commandment. This is known as the Great Commission:

Jesus came and told his disciples, "I have been given all authority in heaven and on earth. Therefore, go and make disciples of all the nations, baptizing them in the name of the Father and the Son and the Holy Spirit. Teach these new disciples to obey all the commands I have given you. And be sure of this: I am with you always, even to the end of the age."

—Matthew 28:18–20 (New Living Translation)

After they are saved, Jesus commands believers to be baptized. Jesus himself was baptized publicly, very early in His ministry. If we are following His commands and His example, we should be baptized too.

The New Testament was originally written in Greek, and the word that we translate into "baptize" in English originally meant "to immerse." That's why most evangelical churches don't merely sprinkle new believers with a few drops of water, but actually immerse them under the surface of the water. Sometimes this takes place in a baptismal pool inside a church. But over the centuries, baptisms have happened in swimming pools, lakes, rivers, bathtubs, hot tubs, and other places.

Jesus was baptized in the Jordan River, and the Bible mentions a voice from heaven—the voice of God—being heard "as Jesus came up out of the water" (Matthew 3:16). Because of this description, we know Jesus wasn't just sprinkled but actually immersed in water for His baptism.

Water baptism, then, is a crucial step after you have received Christ as your Lord and Savior. Jesus did it Himself as an act of obedience to God and as new Christians, we should follow His example. Being water-baptized means we are publicly identifying ourselves with Christ as His followers. It means we are making a declaration of our love and loyalty to Him. It is a public act that signifies a private decision to live for Him, die to our sin, and receive His death as the payment for our rebellious spirit.

Being baptized symbolizes a powerful spiritual truth. God meets us in the water and, because of our obedience, touches our hearts.

As a new believer, you'll will need to find someone to baptize you—even in the current, chaotic state of the post-Rapture world. It could be a fellow believer or a new Christian leader. It could be someone you encounter in an underground church. Your baptism can happen anywhere there is enough water to cover you. All you need is someone to temporarily lower you under the water and say something like: "Because of your profession of faith in the Lord Jesus, I baptize you in the Name of the Father and the Son and the Holy Spirit."

If you can't find anyone to baptize you, then lower yourself into water and say words like this before you go under the water: "As a profession of my faith in Jesus Christ, I am now baptized in the Name of the Father and the Son and the Holy Spirit." It is better to have someone else baptize you if possible and to have other witnesses if they are available. But because of the times you are in right now that might not be possible. The most important thing is that you are making a profession of faith in Jesus. Baptism illustrates the new life you have accepted through Jesus Christ. You are following His example in being baptized. It is your first important step of faith. If you have to baptize yourself for now, maybe later when you are able to meet other believers you can trust, you can then be baptized again publicly. But if that isn't possible, God will honor you for your obedience in taking this important step in your faith.

Some people may acknowledge Jesus intellectually but won't follow through with water baptism because of embarrassment. Maybe they fear the possibility of being rejected or even persecuted by others—and, depending on when you are reading this, you may be living in a very severe period of time in which Christians are being persecuted.

It's not uncommon for a new Christian to fear the social consequences of his or her faith. But this is one of the reasons why Jesus commanded us to be baptized. When He died on the cross for our sins, Jesus was mocked and humiliated. Despite this humiliation, He stayed on the cross. He wasn't ashamed of being identified with us—with sinners—nor was He ashamed of the sins we committed, even as He took that burden on Himself.

So we must ask some important questions:

Will we be too ashamed of Jesus to take the first step of obedience after giving our lives to Him?

Are we going to be private Christians or public Christians?

Are we going to care more about what Jesus thinks about us or what other people think?

You may be living in a time of great confusion and chaos, but if you care more about being accepted by people than about pleasing God, you will be a poor follower of Christ.

Imagine a young groom who wants to marry the bride of his dreams, but is embarrassed to be seen with her at the wedding. "Can't we just get married in secret? There's something about exchanging vows and rings in front of people that makes me feel weird," he might say.

Do you think she'll really want to marry him?

Probably not. She will question whether he really loves her. She will question his commitment to her in the first place.

Remember, *"He who follows Me shall not walk in darkness, but have the light of life"* (John 8:12, New King James Version).

Light is meant to illuminate. As a new believer you are now walking in the light of Jesus Christ. You will need to be wise about how you share your new faith with others. But don't be ashamed of Jesus or afraid of what others may think about your faith. Live your life to please Jesus first and foremost. Jesus was crucified because of His love for you. You must be willing to suffer if necessary to demonstrate your love for Him.

COMMUNION

Baptism is a sacred sign of our relationship with Christ, but it is not the only sign. Another one is communion. You may have heard this called "the Lord's Supper" in some church traditions, or the "Eucharist" in more formal churches.

Water baptism by immersion is a symbol that takes place once at the beginning of our new relationship with Jesus. But communion is an ongoing sign of that relationship. Just like with baptism, Christians take communion because they are following the example of Jesus. Jesus first introduced this to His disciples right before His crucifixion and commanded them to continue it in remembrance of Him.

> *He took some bread and gave thanks to God for it. Then he broke it in pieces and gave it to the disciples, saying, "This is my body, which is given for you. Do this in remembrance of me." After supper he took another cup of wine and said, "This cup is the new covenant between God and his people—an agreement confirmed with my blood, which is poured out as a sacrifice for you."*
> **—Luke 22:19–20 (New Living Translation)**

A generation after Jesus's death and resurrection, the Apostle Paul was teaching a group of Christians who were living in the city of Corinth. He described the significance of communion this way:

> *On the night when he was betrayed, the Lord Jesus took some bread and gave thanks to God for it. Then he broke it in pieces and said, "This is my body, which is given for you. Do this in remembrance of me." In the same way, he*

took the cup of wine after supper, saying, "This cup is the new covenant between God and his people—an agreement confirmed with my blood. Do this in remembrance of me as often as you drink it." For every time you eat this bread and drink this cup, you are announcing the Lord's death until he comes again.

—1 Corinthians 11:23–26 (New Living Translation)

In this passage, Paul is sharing revelation that he received directly from the Lord Himself. He explains that every time we take the bread and the cup—which represent the body and blood of Christ—we are proclaiming the Lord's death. In other words, we are celebrating the freedom Jesus gained for us through His substitutionary death (death for us) on the cross.

Communion helps us remember one of the most important elements of our faith: the love Jesus revealed for us on the cross. That's what the passage above means when it says communion announces "the Lord's death." By taking our place on the cross, He removed the curse of sin from our lives and took it upon His own body. He shed His blood to remove our sins so we could have an eternal and intimate relationship with God. Taking the wine and the bread of communion alone or together with other Christians helps us remember that Jesus died for us and the benefits that are available to us now because of His death and resurrection.

By taking communion, we aren't just eating a piece of bread or drinking a cup of wine or juice. We are receiving the spiritual life and every benefit given us by the death of Jesus. We are remembering His salvation and reflecting on our commitment to Him. What a powerful blessing!

Communion is one of the most sacred traditions of the Christian faith and it has been observed by followers of Jesus since the very first century after His death. When you participate in it, you are participating in a tradition that is as old as Christianity itself.

Before the Rapture, some churches served communion every time they gathered together. Others used to do it once a month. Some churches used actual wine. Others used grape juice. (Both are fine because they symbolize Christ's blood.)

Obviously, this is a very unique time in the history of the world. To be clear, this book was published before the Rapture, which means it was written with a lack of certainty about what things will be like for readers like you. Many churches may no longer be meeting publicly for fear of persecution. They may be meeting secretly or underground. But despite that reality, it is practically guaranteed that, where Christians are gathered together to worship and study, they will somehow be observing communion.

If you are able to join them, please do. You will find communion to be a powerful, spiritual experience. If you can't find other believers, you can take some wine or juice and some bread or crackers and take communion on your own. God will bless you for your obedience in remembering His death.

PART 4

ADDITIONAL STEPS TOWARD CHRIST

Jesus said to the people who believed in him, "You are truly my disciples if you remain faithful to my teachings. And you will know the truth, and the truth will set you free."

—John 8:31–32 (New Living Translation)

Baptism and communion are two of the most important signs and symbols of faith in Jesus Christ, but there are a few other steps of obedience you should know about as a new believer. The first is a type of baptism that differs from immersion in water.

BAPTISM IN THE HOLY SPIRIT

Once when he was eating with them, he commanded them, "Do not leave Jerusalem until the Father sends you the gift he promised, as I told you before. John baptized with water, but in just a few days you will be baptized with the Holy Spirit... But you will receive power when the Holy Spirit comes upon you..."

—Acts 1:4–5,8 (New Living Translation)

Throughout the New Testament, Jesus and other authors regularly describe the Holy Spirit and what He can accomplish in our lives. Jesus often referred to the Holy Spirit as "the Helper," which is a translation of a Greek word, *parakletos*, which means "comforter." It refers to someone who walks alongside us to help us.

In the Book of John, Jesus described this work by the Holy Spirit:

"But the Helper, the Holy Spirit, whom the Father will send in My name, He will teach you all things, and bring to your remembrance all things that I said to you."

—John 14:26 (New King James Version)

"When the Spirit of truth comes, he will guide you into all truth. He will not speak on his own but will tell you what he has heard. He will tell you about the future. He will bring me glory by telling you whatever he receives from me."

—John 16:13–14 (New Living Translation)

One of the most intriguing ways the New Testament talks about the Holy Spirit is its descriptions of something called the Baptism of the Holy Spirit. In the passage from the book of Acts and chapter 1, Jesus told the disciples to wait in Jerusalem until the Holy Spirit empowered them to be His witnesses on earth. According to Jesus, the Holy Spirit would give them power when they are baptized into Him. He said this to His followers forty days after His resurrection and right before He ascended into heaven.

Ten days later, at the Feast of Pentecost, it happened. The Holy Spirit descended on a group of believers all at once, transforming their lives. The Book of Acts describes it like this:

> *On the day of Pentecost all the believers were meeting together in one place. Suddenly, there was a sound from heaven like the roaring of a mighty windstorm, and it filled the house where they were sitting. Then, what looked like flames or tongues of fire appeared and settled on each of them. And everyone present was filled with the Holy Spirit and began speaking in other languages, as the Holy Spirit gave them this ability. At that time there were devout Jews from every nation living in Jerusalem. When they heard the loud noise, everyone came running, and they were bewildered to hear their own languages being spoken by the believers.*
>
> **—Acts 2:1–6 (New Living Translation)**

Some foreigners who were present for this event heard the group speaking in their own, familiar languages and worshiped God because of this miracle. They praised Him because of the wonderful things He had done. But others ridiculed them and suggested that they were drunk.

Peter, one of the disciples, defended these Christians who had been filled by the Holy Spirit. Peter referred to an Old Testament passage from the book of Joel about the end times:

> *'In the last days,' God says,*
>> *I will pour out my Spirit upon all people.*
>
> *Your sons and daughters will prophesy.*
>> *Your young men will see visions,*
>> *and your old men will dream dreams.*
>
> *In those days I will pour out my Spirit*
>> *even on my servants—men and women alike—*
>> *and they will prophesy.*
>
> *And I will cause wonders in the heavens above*
>> *and signs on the earth below—*
>> *blood and fire and clouds of smoke.*
>
> *The sun will become dark,*
>> *and the moon will turn blood red*
>> *before that great and glorious day of the Lord arrives.*
>
> *But everyone who calls on the name of the Lord*
>> *will be saved.'*

—Acts 2:17–21 (New Living Translation)

That day, a large number of Christ-followers were immersed into an empowering relationship with the Holy Spirit so they could better know and serve God. The

Holy Spirit is God and is equal with God the Son (Jesus) and God the Father. You may hear all three referred to at once as the Trinity. Because all three are equal, the Holy Spirit always speaks and acts in accordance with the nature of God and the Word of God.

These believers had already trusted Jesus by the time the Holy Spirit descended upon them. Some in the group were His original disciples! They had previously given their lives to Christ.

For many faithful Christians, baptism in the Holy Spirit is an experience that happens after salvation. Every believer has been born again by the Holy Spirit, but a full immersion into His fullness—the empowerment to know and serve God—is a separate, unique experience. It may happen a few minutes after you say a prayer like the one shared in this book. It may happen days, months or even years after you give your heart to Jesus.

But it doesn't happen automatically because we are saved.

Being saved is about accepting Jesus's lordship. It is about forgiveness of sins and the gift of eternal life. Baptism in the Holy Spirit, however, is about living for God in this life and enjoying the powerful assistance of God every day to know Him, overcome sin, and accomplish His will. We cannot do these things on our own. We must have the continual partnership of the Holy Spirit. That is why Jesus spoke of Him so often and commanded the disciples to wait for Him to descend upon them in power.

A daily, dependent relationship with the Holy Spirit is absolutely necessary in the life of a believer. Look at it this way: Salvation is taking a drink of living water that resurrects the spirit inside of you. Baptism in the Holy Spirit is jumping into the lake where that living water comes from. It is a full immersion that empowers your total being.

The best way to receive the Holy Spirit is to ask a Spirit-filled believer to lay their hands on you and pray for you to be baptized in the Spirit. This was the primary manner the Holy Spirit came upon believers in the Bible.

But if you don't know other believers or those you know don't understand about the Holy Spirt, you can receive Him by simply asking God and receiving Him by faith—just as you received Jesus when you were saved. The Spirit is a free gift from God. You can say a simple prayer like this to receive Him: *Lord, I ask You to baptize me in Your Holy Spirit and to fill me with the power to live for You. Holy Spirit, I need You in my life to be able to live victoriously for Jesus. Baptize me now and be my daily Helper to comfort, teach, and empower me to live for God. I receive You by faith as a free gift. In Jesus' Name amen!*

CHRISTIAN FRIENDSHIP

As iron sharpens iron, so a friend sharpens a friend.
—**Proverbs 27:17 (New Living Translation)**

Because of the uncertainty of the post-Rapture world you will be living in when you read this book, writing this section of the book is a challenge. It is very difficult to imagine what to expect. It is very difficult to know how easy—or how hard—it will be to find other Christian believers during this time.

But finding those believers is essential. Finding a way to gather with those believers is extremely important. Without a committed relationship with other new Christians, it will be a great challenge to get through the next few years on earth. It will also be a special challenge to sustain your newfound faith—but the Holy Spirit will be with you regardless of what you must endure.

Choosing your friends carefully matters. Time and time again in the world before the Rapture, Christians would step away from faith or fall into sin because of unhealthy relationships. It doesn't matter how intelligent or wonderful they were as individuals. It doesn't matter how talented, mature, or dedicated they were. If they end up influenced by the wrong crowd, their faith is in danger. Inevitably, they will fail spiritually if they don't change.

Here is a truth you should remember for the rest of your life: *You will always become like the people closest to you.*

In 1 Corinthians 15:33, the Apostle Paul put it this way: "Bad company corrupts good character (New Living Translation)."

He starts with the negative. When you are in close relationship ("company") with someone, the negative has greater power than the positive. Imagine you are standing on a platform, and you clasp hands with a person standing below you. It will be far easier for them to pull you down to their level than it will be for you to pull them up onto your platform.

Bad company will corrupt your good intentions. Bad company will defile your good habits. Navigating the world you are living in today will be very difficult and you will likely have to rely on others, but be very careful with those relationships. It will be extremely easy to fall into a relationship that harms your faith, especially when you link up with people who are not actively living as Christians.

Paul describes the danger of this scenario in this passage:

> *Don't team up with those who are unbelievers. How can righteousness be a partner with wickedness? How can light live with darkness? What harmony can there be between Christ and the devil? How can a believer be a partner with an unbeliever? And what union can there be between God's temple and idols? For we are the temple of the living God. As God said:*
> *"I will live in them*
> *and walk among them.*
> *I will be their God,*
> *and they will be my people.*
> *Therefore, come out from among unbelievers,*
> *and separate yourselves from them," says the LORD.*

> *"Don't touch their filthy things,*
> *and I will welcome you.*
> *And I will be your Father,*
> *and you will be my sons and daughters,*
> *says the Lord Almighty."*
> —2 Corinthians 6:14–18 (New Living Translation)

In the original Greek language of this text, the word translated as "team up" refers to an old agricultural technique in which a farming implement—a yoke—binds together two cattle or oxen for the task of plowing. The two creatures have to move together, in the same direction, in order to accomplish any work. If they try to move in different directions, they won't be able to move at all.

Paul uses this metaphor to warn his readers that Christians should not be engaged in entangling, binding relationships with those who are not believers. This includes all close relationships, including marriage. That is not to say you should abandon your spouse if both of you were left behind after the Rapture but only one of you has given their life to Jesus Christ. You should remain married. You need each other now more than ever before. But be very aware of the influence a nonbeliever can have on a believer.

All of us know people in our families or neighborhoods from the "before" time, people at school or at work who regularly displayed negative, unrighteous behavior. Those people need Jesus and need friends. They need love. However, they cannot be the source of your closest friendship.

If at all possible, try to seek out other new believers in Christ, people who share your values and commitment. Then, from that foundation, you can reach out to others without worrying about them having a negative influence on you.

One more Bible passage shares about this:

> *Let us think of ways to motivate one another to acts of love and good works. And let us not neglect our meeting together, as some people do, but encourage one another, especially now that the day of his return is drawing near.*
> **—Hebrews 10:24–25 (New Living Translation)**

This is a very important text of Scripture. It encourages us to meet on a regular basis with other believers and tells us exactly why we should do so: Because we need to stir one another up to love God and serve others. We need to uplift each other to serve the Lord faithfully, especially "now that the day of his return is drawing near."

If you are reading this after the Rapture, the day of Christ's return is nearer than ever.

You are living in an evil world right now. This is the most chaotic and dreadful time in human history. God created you to live in community and to gain strength from relationships, so you need the constant love and encouragement of friendships with other Christians.

Without it, you may find it very difficult to endure the temptation, deception, and persecution of these days.

But with strong, Christian relationships, you can keep the faith. You can hold strong to your commitment to Jesus. You can make a difference in the lives of others and even lead others to a relationship with Christ. That is the highest purpose of your new life as a believer.

CHURCH IN THE POST-RAPTURE WORLD

Related to the topic of Christian friendships and gathering with other believers, you may have a preexisting opinion about church as you understood it before the Rapture. You may even have attended a church from time to time.

If so, it is likely you have a perspective on church that will need to adjust in relation to the society that has been left behind. Before, in some cities and communities, many churches were large gatherings of hundreds or even thousands of people. They had enormous buildings and dynamic stages. They offered comfortable seating, professional audio/video equipment, and the teams of ministers and volunteers necessary to pull off an impressive service every Sunday.

"Church" may never look like that again.

That's okay, because the church services you are remembering themselves were very different from church services that took place in the 1800s, or from as far back as the 1400s. And those church gatherings were very different from the way Christians met during the first century, only a few years removed from the death and resurrection of Jesus Christ.

Those early believers didn't meet in fancy buildings. They didn't have professional lighting or video projection. They didn't sit in pews or have stained glass windows. For the most part, they didn't even have paid preachers or ministers. They didn't even have Bibles, at least as we think of the Bible today. The earliest gatherings of Christian believers took place in people's homes or outdoors. These new Christians would simply meet together, sing some songs of worship, read Scripture in the form of scrolls or letters, and pray together. That was church for them.

That may be church for you as well.

Today's megachurch buildings may all be empty. That's not a bad thing. They served their purpose in the world before the Rapture, and the fact that they have fallen out of use testifies to the faith of their members.

The churches of today may be much less flamboyant. For one thing, after all the world's Christians were removed from the earth, it will take time for a new generation of Christians to rise up. Most in this new generation will be like you—new believers who have encountered a book like this or a Bible, or people who have met someone who recently gave their lives to Christ. Slowly but surely, the Christian Church will rebuild.

As it does, gatherings of Christians will increase. These gatherings may be taking place out of the public eye, in basements of homes, or in other abandoned buildings. As persecution and violence increase in these days—which the Bible predicts—these gatherings will definitely be held in secret. To find them, ask around. Remember, almost every believer you meet will be a new Christian, just like you. You need each other, so seek out these new believers. You will provide each other friendship, comfort, and prayer.

Jesus had encouraging words for small groups of believers:

"For where two or three gather together as my followers, I am there among them."

—Matthew 18:20 (New Living Translation)

We experience God in a powerful way when we gather together with other Christians, even if it's just two or three believers praying or singing together. These gatherings are essential. Ask God to help you find someone else who shares your commitment to Christ. He will answer that prayer because that is what He wants for you.

THE IMPORTANCE OF SCRIPTURE

Your word is a lamp to guide my feet and a light for my path.

—Psalm 119:105 (New Living Translation)

You have probably already noticed how frequently this book refers to verses from the Bible, and how much the teaching in these pages relies on the Bible. That's because the Bible is God's Word and the essence and standard of all truth.

Now that you are a believer in Christ, it is essential that you build a daily discipline into your life to read Scripture on a regular basis. The Holy Spirit inspired the authors of the Bible and will help you understand it as you read. That is one reason the baptism of the Holy Spirit is so important for a believer. As Jesus told the disciples in John 16:13, *"when the Spirit of truth comes, he will guide you into all truth"* (New Living Translation).

Many believers have found it a helpful practice to read the Bible for 15 or 20 minutes a day, allowing the Word to minister to them, educate them, and empower them to live for Christ. Reading and knowing God's Word, the Bible, is critical in building a relationship with the Lord and learning how to live for Him.

It is especially important during times like these. As a new follower of Jesus, you need to know the Word. It will give you strength to endure the difficulties of this world. But how can you know the Bible unless you immerse yourself in it?

As mentioned in an earlier chapter of this book, one of the most important things you need to do right now is to locate a Bible somewhere. You might have one already. Though not everyone in the pre-Rapture world followed Jesus, the Bible has always been the number-one selling book in the world. Many nonbelievers likely had Bibles in their homes, forgotten, or ignored somewhere on a dusty bookshelf.

If you don't have a Bible, again, it should be fairly easy to find one in an abandoned home or an empty business, church, or hotel. There is a good chance that you can find a Bible located near the place where you first discovered this book. When you find a Bible, take it for yourself. Don't worry about it originally having been someone else's property. If the original owner has been raptured, he or she would definitely want you to have it—especially if you are planning to read it and learn from it. You may also be able to download a Bible on your phone or tablet or to read one on your computer. You will need to be wise if you are using an electronic version of the Bible to make sure you are not being tracked by those who will be persecuting believers.

Find a Bible, because there are three crucial roles the Bible plays in the life of a believer:

1. It renews our minds to think as we should

Don't copy the behavior and customs of this world, but let God transform you into a new person by changing the way you think. Then you will learn to know God's will for you, which is good and pleasing and perfect.
—Romans 12:2 (New Living Translation)

If you have spent any time at all using computers or smart devices, you know that these contain hardware and software. The metal and glass and silicon of the devices themselves represent the hardware. The apps and programs and operating systems that empower them are the software.

Humans are similar. We have been equipped by God with incredible hardware—our bodies and brains. However, we have serious software problems.

Sin is like a virus that has been downloaded into our hearts and corrupted our software. Our selfish, sinful nature hinders our relationship with God and warps our relationships with each other. This sin nature has spread from one device to another—from one human generation to the next—and the result is the chaos and evil you see in the world today.

God has given us a gift in the wonder of our bodies and brains, but it doesn't matter how awesome the hardware is if the software doesn't run correctly. For a Christian, reading the Bible is like running one of those programs designed to wipe a virus off a hard drive and restore the device to the way it is supposed to work.

The book of Psalm chapter 1 even says that those who meditate on God's Word day and night will find success in everything they do. What a powerful promise! Everything in our lives will succeed by simply "downloading" God's Word into our minds and allowing it to guide us and transform us.

In fact, you have never read a book as powerful as the Bible:

For the word of God is alive and powerful. It is sharper than the sharpest two-edged sword, cutting between soul and spirit, between joint and marrow. It exposes our innermost thoughts and desires.

—Hebrews 4:12 (New Living Translation)

The Bible is more than just pages and ink. It is alive. As you read it, Scripture fills your spirit with the light of God. It goes to war against sin and evil, hacking away at these things like a "two-edged sword." It goes where no human being could ever go and accomplishes things no human force could ever do. It examines every thought and intent of the heart and removes anything that is harmful.

Reading God's Word every day will transform your heart and mind.

2. It creates intimacy with God

In the beginning the Word already existed. The Word was with God, and the Word was God. He existed in the beginning with God. God created everything through him, and nothing was created except through him. The Word gave life to everything that was created, and his life brought light to everyone.

—John 1:1–4 (New Living Translation)

This text is the opening of the Book of John and one of the most important passages in the Bible, because it reveals Jesus as "the Word." It tells us He is God and the Creator of all things, the perfect living portrayal of the truth of God. Jesus is the embodiment of everything the Bible has to say.

It is important to remember this as you read Scripture. The Word is not some*thing*. It is some*one*. The Bible is the revelation of Jesus.

Another important passage from the Bible makes this clear:

> *All Scripture is inspired by God and is useful to teach us what is true and to make us realize what is wrong in our lives. It corrects us when we are wrong and teaches us to do what is right. God uses it to prepare and equip his people to do every good work.*
>
> **—2 Timothy 3:16–17 (New Living Translation)**

Remember, the New Testament was originally written in ancient Greek. The words we translate "inspired by God" from this passage originally meant "breathed by God." In other words, all of the Bible is God-breathed and life-giving. It comes directly from God! When we read it, we aren't just learning information or taking in ancient stories. We are experiencing someone: the Creator of the Universe. The Giver of all Good Things. The Almighty God.

That's why, when you read the Bible, you will find that it causes you to feel more alive than before. You will feel stronger mentally and spiritually. When you read

God's Word, you will encounter God. He meets you there. He speaks to you, encourages you, loves you and comforts you. He becomes real through His Word and your relationship to Him grows closer the more time you spend in the Word.

You will find that you need that connection more than ever in these dark days.

Jesus once said this about His words: *"The very words I have spoken to you are spirit and life"* (John 6:63, New Living Translation).

When you dedicate yourself to reading the Bible and rely on the Holy Spirit for guidance, you will discover a deeper, more profound spiritual life. You will enjoy a more vibrant, intimate, and personal relationship with the Lord. It is simply not possible to know Him intimately apart from His Word.

3. It empowers us for victory

A final word: Be strong in the Lord and in his mighty power. Put on all of God's armor so that you will be able to stand firm against all strategies of the devil. For we are not fighting against flesh-and-blood enemies, but against evil rulers and authorities of the unseen world, against mighty powers in this dark world, and against evil spirits in the heavenly places.

Therefore, put on every piece of God's armor so you will be able to resist the enemy in the time of evil. Then after the battle you will still be standing firm.

Stand your ground, putting on the belt of truth and the body armor of God's righteousness. For shoes, put on the peace that comes from the Good News so that you will be fully prepared. In addition to all of these, hold up the shield of faith to stop the fiery arrows of the devil. Put on salvation as your helmet, and take the sword of the Spirit, which is the word of God.

—Ephesians 6:10–17 (New Living Translation)

The Apostle Paul wrote this text to make sure the early Church knew that their true enemies were not ungodly human authorities or rulers, but adversaries in the invisible realm. So often we think our biggest problems are with people we know, politicians we disagree with, or even nations that are in conflict with us. Today, you may even feel like your enemies are everywhere. But none of those things are true.

Our most serious enemies are spiritual enemies.

One of the most important realities we must be aware of is the presence of evil forces, under the control of Satan, sent to keep us from fulfilling God's will for our lives. Paul writes in this passage in Ephesians that evil is real, and our true adversaries are not "flesh and blood." We can defend ourselves against this unseen, demonic enemy by putting on the spiritual armor God has given us to defend ourselves.

Ultimately, Jesus has already defeated the devil by dying on the cross and rising again. He has given us victory. This is a huge blessing every believer needs to understand. However, we also have to remember victory each day isn't automatic just because we are believers. We have to rely on the authority God has given us in order to succeed and live as we should.

Take note of the weapons listed in the Ephesians chapter 6 passage above: a shield, a helmet, body armor, shoes, and a belt. These are defensive weapons. The entire list is defensive against the "fiery arrows" of the enemy, except for one: the sword of the Spirit, which represents the Word of God. The Bible is an offensive weapon. The Word is our sword, and its truth strikes a deathblow against every force that comes against us.

In one famous passage of the Bible, in Matthew chapter 4, Jesus is tempted by the devil in the wilderness. Jesus gains victory not through violence or force but by quoting God's Word. The entire "battle" is an exchange of words and passages of Scripture. Whenever the devil tries to tempt Jesus with a half-truth, Jesus quotes Scripture and, in doing so, defeats the devil. In the realm of the spirit, the Word of God represents the most powerful nuclear weapon in the universe. One Scripture spoken in faith can vanquish the powers of hell.

The devil may come to you attempting to overwhelm you with doubt, fear, condemnation, confusion, and lies. He will bring deception and temptation to try to defeat you. As a result, you may face negative and destructive thoughts from time to time. These are the "fiery arrows" of the devil. You can protect yourself with the armor of God and strike back against them with the Bible. All you need to do is find a Scripture that fits your circumstances and quote it back to the devil, just as Jesus did.

With God's Word, you can win any battle. Scripture is God's power that works within us. All we have to do is read it, believe it, and confess it.

PART 5

WHAT HAPPENS NEXT
IN THE WORLD?

The sun will become dark, and the moon will turn blood red before that great and terrible day of the LORD arrives.

—Joel 2:31 (New Living Translation)

The message of the Gospel is good news. Literally, the word *gospel* comes from an old Anglo-Saxon word that means "good news." Jesus paid the price for your sin and offers you the free gift of salvation, securing your place in God's Kingdom and promising an eternity in His presence, in heaven. If you have decided to give your life to Jesus, you have made the most important decision you will ever make in your lifetime.

That is indeed good news.

But this chapter represents the "bad news" portion of this book. Now that the Rapture has occurred, the world has been thrust into violence, chaos, and confusion. Likely by the time you read this, that chaos has intensified. Things are getting worse and worse. Governments are failing and society has been greatly disrupted. Social services are breaking down. Utilities may be failing. Buildings are abandoned and the streets seem unsafe.

This moment may already be difficult for you, but it is only going to get worse.

According to the Bible, the time you are living in now is called "the Tribulation." Jesus spoke about it in Matthew 24:

> *"For there will be greater anguish than at any time since the world began. And it will never be so great again. In fact, unless that time of calamity is shortened, not a single person will survive. But it will be shortened for the sake of God's chosen ones."*
>
> **—Matthew 24:21–22 (New Living Translation)**

In that context, "God's chosen ones" now includes you as a new believer. This time will be terrible, but God will limit its length for you and other Christians. The Bible says the Tribulation period will last for seven years.

The most important thing you need to know right now is that, after the seven years are over, you will no longer have an opportunity to repent and be saved. Hopefully you have already made that choice to follow Jesus.

If not, you need to turn back the pages in this book and make that decision now because this fallen world will make it harder and harder for you to follow Jesus as the days go by. If you think things are bad now, the Bible says the last half of the Tribulation—the final three-and-a-half years—will be even worse than it is now.

Today is the day to accept His gift of salvation so you can be in God's presence forever. Don't wait! There will never be a better time to do so than right now. At the end of the seven-year Tribulation, you will be joined forever with Jesus.

If you don't repent and ask Jesus to be Lord of your life—if you deny Christ—you will go to hell for eternity.

WHAT IS THE TRIBULATION?

They have power to shut the sky so that no rain will fall for as long as they prophesy. And they have the power to turn the rivers and oceans into blood, and to strike the earth with every kind of plague as often as they wish.
—Revelation 11:6 (New Living Translation)

The Rapture set in motion a timeline for the last days of humanity that was predicted thousands of years ago in the Bible. When God removed the Church—His believers—through the Rapture, He was protecting them from experiencing what the Bible calls His "wrath" (1 Thessalonians 5:9). That wrath represents God's holy anger directed at a world of sin and rebellion. The

Tribulation will be the period during which God unleashes His wrath on the earth as a form of judgment.

Scholars and theologians refer to this period as the Tribulation because that is the word Jesus used when telling His disciples about the last days in The Book of Matthew chapter 24. The King James Version of the Bible translates the original Greek term as "tribulation." Other versions use the words *calamity* or *persecution* or *anguish*:

> *"For there will be greater anguish than at any time since the world began. And it will never be so great again."*
> —Matthew 24:21 (New Living Translation)

Regardless of the word used, the Tribulation reflects the most dangerous and distressing time in human history—and, in fact, the final seven years of human history. Because the Rapture has already happened and Christian believers have disappeared, you can assume that the Tribulation has begun.

Your world has probably already been plagued with outbreaks of violence and devastation. Rest assured: It is going to get worse. Society will deteriorate beyond even what you have experienced already.

THE ANTICHRIST

If you still have access to worldwide news broadcasts, you may have heard about a peace treaty. The Bible says the Tribulation would begin after the Rapture with the confirming of a peace treaty between Israel and an individual described in Scripture as "the Antichrist" and "the Beast." This individual likely will not refer to himself this way. He will be human and will have a name, just like any of us. But he will have emerged as a great global leader. He is probably a very charismatic and charming person. The Bible says he will be a male.

Depending on when you read this book, you may already know exactly who this individual is. It is also possible he may still be in the process of coming to power. Regardless, it will soon be clear that this man is the most evil person to have walked the earth. Here are a few ways the Bible describes him:

Despicable: *The next to come to power will be a despicable man who is not in line for royal succession. He will slip in when least expected and take over the kingdom by flattery and intrigue.*

—Daniel 11:21 (New Living Translation)

A Blasphemer: *The king will do as he pleases, exalting himself and claiming to be greater than every god, even blaspheming the God of gods. He will succeed, but only until the time of wrath is completed. For what has been determined will surely take place.*

—Daniel 11:36 (New Living Translation)

Destructive and Lawless: *For that day will not come until there is a great rebellion against God and the man of lawlessness is revealed—the one who brings destruction. He will exalt himself and defy everything that people call god and every object of worship. He will even sit in the temple of God, claiming that he himself is God.*

—2 Thessalonians 2:3–4 (New Living Translation)

The Beast: *When they complete their testimony, the beast that comes up out of the bottomless pit will declare war against them, and he will conquer them and kill them.*

—Revelation 11:7 (New Living Translation)

In one of the passages above, in the Book of 2 Thessalonians, the Apostle Paul describes the Antichrist as the "man of lawlessness." This comes from a Greek word, *anomia*, that means having a contempt for the law. It was used back then to describe someone who willingly violates the law.

In other words, Paul is describing a person who knowingly and intentionally opposes God's law. The Antichrist may be a powerful, charming leader, but he will also be manipulative. Even worse, he will stand in opposition to God's Word as we understand it from the Bible. He will directly disobey the Word of God.

The Antichrist will be diametrically opposed to God and His Son, Jesus Christ. He may promise peace and even bring peace on a temporary basis—because of the peace treaty with Israel—but this will be a counterfeit peace. It is based on a lie, and it won't last.

THE FIRST HALF OF THE TRIBULATION

The first half of the Tribulation, after the Rapture and the peace treaty of the Antichrist, will be dominated by the ministry of two people the Bible refers to as the "two witnesses" or the "two prophets." These are two individuals God will use to accomplish His work while the Antichrist rises to political and military power.

The Bible doesn't identify them by name. Before the Rapture, scholars and theologians tried to identify who they might be and speculated that they could be the return of biblical figures like Elijah or Enoch. By this point, you may know who they are, by name.

God will have given miraculous powers to these two witnesses, and they will gain the world's attention at the same time the Antichrist is rising to political and military power. It should be easy for you to understand and identify who these two individuals might be.

The Bible says God will spiritually empower these two witnesses, who will preach His word boldly and will do great signs and wonders for the world to see. Here is what the Book of Revelation says about them:

> *These two prophets are the two olive trees and the two lampstands that stand before the Lord of all the earth. If*

anyone tries to harm them, fire flashes from their mouths and consumes their enemies. This is how anyone who tries to harm them must die. They have power to shut the sky so that no rain will fall for as long as they prophesy. And they have the power to turn the rivers and oceans into blood, and to strike the earth with every kind of plague as often as they wish.

—Revelation 11:4–6 (New Living Translation)

Despite these incredible powers, the Beast of Revelation—the godless Antichrist—will eventually kill the two witnesses in a very public way. It will capture the world's attention. When he does, the unsaved world will celebrate:

When they complete their testimony, the beast that comes up out of the bottomless pit will declare war against them, and he will conquer them and kill them. And their bodies will lie in the main street of Jerusalem, the city that is figuratively called "Sodom" and "Egypt," the city where their Lord was crucified. And for three and a half days, all peoples, tribes, languages, and nations will stare at their bodies. No one will be allowed to bury them. All the people who belong to this world will gloat over them and give presents to each other to celebrate the death of the two prophets who had tormented them.

—Revelation 11:7–10 (New Living Translation)

Then, while everyone rejoices over their death, the two witnesses will be resurrected right in front of the entire world, convincing many of the power of God. This miracle will also be accompanied by a devastating, deadly catastrophe:

> *But after three and a half days, God breathed life into them, and they stood up! Terror struck all who were staring at them. Then a loud voice from heaven called to the two prophets, "Come up here!" And they rose to heaven in a cloud as their enemies watched. At the same time there was a terrible earthquake that destroyed a tenth of the city. Seven thousand people died in that earthquake, and everyone else was terrified and gave glory to the God of heaven.*
>
> —Revelation 11:11–13 (New Living Translation)

During the ministry of the two witnesses, the Antichrist will slowly be gaining power and influence in the world. He will begin to rise to prominence soon after the Rapture and eventually set himself up as a replacement for Jesus Christ.

Again, this may be happening now, or it may have already happened by the time you read this. Regardless, you need to take extreme caution because of what is coming next.

According to God's Word, the Antichrist will eventually place an image of himself in the Temple in Jerusalem and demand that the world worship this image. In addition to this blatant blasphemy, he will also try to force every single human to allow some kind of mark on the hand or forehead. This mark, described in the Bible as the "Mark of the Beast," will allow individuals to buy, sell, and take part in the world's economy. Without it, they will be shut out from most of society.

This mark will be the primary way the Antichrist controls the world. He will have ascended into military and political power, but his true control comes from financial power. Once he controls the act of buying and selling across the world, that financial power will give him ultimate authority over every society and country remaining on earth.

Because this book is being written prior to the Rapture and the Tribulation, it is impossible to describe the details of this mark. Some people have speculated it might be a barcode, a microchip, or some kind of tattoo. We only know the mark won't be optional.

If you want to conduct business of any kind, you will be required to have the Mark of the Beast. But it should be avoided at all costs! Do not worship the Antichrist and do not take his mark. If you do, you will be subject of God's wrath. Here is what the Bible says about it:

> *Then a third angel followed them, shouting, "Anyone who worships the beast and his statue or who accepts his mark on the forehead or on the hand must drink the wine of God's anger. It has been poured full strength into God's cup of wrath. And they will be tormented with fire and burning sulfur in the presence of the holy angels and the Lamb. The smoke of their torment will rise forever and*

ever, and they will have no relief day or night, for they have worshiped the beast and his statue and have accepted the mark of his name." This means that God's holy people must endure persecution patiently, obeying his commands and maintaining their faith in Jesus.

—Revelation 14:9–12 (New Living Translation)

The mark itself—whatever it might be—isn't just about having the individual ability to buy or sell, based on the rules set by the Antichrist. Accepting the mark is also a form of accepting the godless ideology of the Beast. It is a personal alignment with the Antichrist, against God. That is why this sin is unforgivable. That is why it will be met with God's wrath. You cannot be forgiven. Once you accept it, you will be giving yourself over to an eternity in hell.

But refusing the mark will result in another kind of temporary trouble. According to the Bible, all those who refuse the mark will be persecuted. They may even be killed.

It will be extremely difficult to avoid the mark. But for the sake of your faith in Christ and your eternal soul, you must reject the mark of the Beast.

THE SECOND HALF OF THE TRIBULATION

Already the Tribulation period sounds very bad, but the most intense part of this time will be the second half—the last three-and-a-half years that are referred to as "The Great Tribulation." Obviously, you are living right now in a very traumatic period of human history, regardless of whether the Rapture occurred a few days ago or whether it was weeks, months, or even years ago. These are the darkest days that the earth has ever seen.

You can take comfort that God is with you, and He will give you strength as you depend upon Him.

But do not lose sight of the fact that the Antichrist—who may have already come to power—is literally the devil incarnate. He is the most evil person in the history of the world. He hates God and hates God's Word. He will also hate believers and those who refuse to take his mark or worship him.

Being a believer in Christ during this time will require extreme commitment and courage. It could very well cost your life. The Bible describes multiple plagues and judgments impacting the earth during the Tribulation. Some are natural catastrophes like earthquakes or fires. Others are supernatural and demonic. There will be sickness, death, and destruction. Famine and severe weather will become commonplace. Nation will rise against nation. Families will be torn apart from strife.

Meanwhile, the Antichrist will kill millions of people who refuse to worship him because they have chosen to put their faith in Jesus.

The Antichrist will come to power during the first three-and-a-half years of the Tribulation, after the Rapture. This will also be the period when the two witnesses are prophesying. But after their death, the Antichrist (the Beast) will be given full reign over the world. This passage of Scripture describes the second half of the Tribulation in very ominous language:

> *Then the beast was allowed to speak great blasphemies against God. And he was given authority to do whatever he wanted for forty-two months. And he spoke terrible words of blasphemy against God, slandering his name and his dwelling—that is, those who dwell in heaven. And the beast was allowed to wage war against God's holy people and to conquer them. And he was given authority to rule over every tribe and people and language and nation. And all the people who belong to this world worshiped the beast. They are the ones whose names were not written in the Book of Life that belongs to the Lamb who was slaughtered before the world was made.*
>
> *Anyone with ears to hear*
> *should listen and understand.*
> *Anyone who is destined for prison*
> *will be taken to prison.*
> *Anyone destined to die by the sword*
> *will die by the sword.*
> *This means that God's holy people must endure persecution patiently and remain faithful.*
>
> **—Revelation 13:5–10 (New Living Translation)**

This information isn't meant to frighten you, but to warn you about what is coming. You need to be informed about the present situation and aware of the dark days that are ahead, so you can prepare yourself to endure persecution and remain faithful despite the hardships coming your way.

Christians have been discussing these passages for hundreds of years, and now these events are being fulfilled. The world is being severely judged by God because of humanity's sins and rejection of Jesus, but it won't last forever.

In fact, this severe period of judgment will only last for seven years.

The Tribulation is not the end of the story.

PART 6

IS THERE ANY HOPE?

"Look, I am coming soon, bringing my reward with me to repay all people according to their deeds. I am the Alpha and the Omega, the First and the Last, the Beginning and the End."

—Revelation 22:12–13 (New Living Translation)

The seven years of the Tribulation will be the most terrible, horrific years the planet has ever seen. This period will be marked by abominations, disasters, death, and disease as God judges the world for its sin. That's the very bad news of the Bible and this book.

The good news is that the darkness will not last, because Jesus is returning.

Yes, there is hope.

One of the most important doctrines taught throughout the Bible is that of the Second Coming of Jesus. He arrived first in the world as a baby. His birth was prophesied long before a human infant was born to Mary and Joseph in a stable near the town of Bethlehem. The circumstances of His birth were humble. He entered the world as the child of a young woman. His birth was first announced to working-class shepherds. The first coming of Jesus—the Christmas story—was incredibly meaningful but quiet and unassuming.

The Second Coming will be different. It will be public. It will be dramatic. It will not take place in a rustic stable but in the skies above, with power and glory and the sound of trumpets. The Book of Titus in the New Testament describes the Second Coming as *"... that wonderful day when the glory of our great God and Savior, Jesus Christ, will be revealed"* (Titus 2:13, New Living Translation).

Jesus described His Second Coming to His disciples right after He informed them about the anguish of the Tribulation:

> *"Immediately after the anguish of those days,*
>> *the sun will be darkened,*
>>> *the moon will give no light,*
>>> *the stars will fall from the sky,*
>>>> *and the powers in the heavens will be shaken.*
> *And then at last, the sign that the Son of Man is coming will appear in the heavens, and there will be deep mourning among all the peoples of the earth. And they will see the Son of Man coming on the clouds of heaven with power and great glory. And he will send out his*

angels with the mighty blast of a trumpet, and they will gather his chosen ones from all over the world—from the farthest ends of the earth and heaven."
—Matthew 24:29–31 (New Living Translation)

Accompanied by His angels, Jesus will return this time as a conqueror and eternal king. He will destroy sin and death. At that time, all those who committed their lives to Him during the Tribulation—a number that, hopefully, now includes you—will be gathered to Him from all over the world. Those who are still living will be raptured, just like so many others were a few years earlier.

The disappearance of millions of Christians during the Rapture was a private event between Jesus and the Church. That's why you had so many questions about it. It happened in an instant, without fanfare or explanation. The word's believers were here one day and then, without warning, they were gone—in the twinkling of an eye.

The Rapture was selective and instantaneous.

But the Second Coming will be an extremely public event. It will happen in real-time, and during the Second Coming, every eye will see Jesus. The entire earth will watch Jesus come out of the clouds in glory. Those who know Him will rejoice. But those who do not know Him—those who took the Mark of the Beast and worshipped the Antichrist—will have the opposite response.

Revelation chapter 19 describes this moment. The passage mentions Heaven opening and Jesus arriving on a white horse to wage "a righteous war" against the Beast and the kings of the world. Accompanying Him are all the angelic forces of the heavenly realm. What a sight this will be!

> *The armies of heaven, dressed in the finest of pure white linen, followed him on white horses. From his mouth came a sharp sword to strike down the nations. He will rule them with an iron rod. He will release the fierce wrath of God, the Almighty, like juice flowing from a winepress.*
> —Revelation 19:14–15 (New Living Translation)

Whether you grew up with knowledge of the Bible or not, you probably think of Jesus as a kind, compassionate and humble teacher. There are hymns about Jesus being "meek and mild." This perspective is accurate, because Jesus loves you more than you'll ever understand. He is patient, kind, and tenderhearted.

That's why He has given humanity so many centuries to hear His teachings and follow Him. But when Jesus returns in the Second Coming, He is also coming as the Great Judge. He will release the fierce wrath of God upon unbelievers at the worst moment in the history of the world.

Another Bible prophecy says that His return will be centered upon the Mount of Olives in Jerusalem, splitting this historic city into two parts. The impact will be instant. Night will become day and He will become King over all the earth:

Watch, for the day of the Lord is coming when your possessions will be plundered right in front of you! I will gather all the nations to fight against Jerusalem. The city will be taken, the houses looted, and the women raped. Half the population will be taken into captivity, and the rest will be left among the ruins of the city. Then the Lord will go out to fight against those nations, as he has fought in times past. On that day his feet will stand on the Mount of Olives, east of Jerusalem. And the Mount of Olives will split apart, making a wide valley running from east to west. Half the mountain will move toward the north and half toward the south. You will flee through this valley, for it will reach across to Azal. Yes, you will flee as you did from the earthquake in the days of King Uzziah of Judah. Then the Lord my God will come, and all his holy ones with him.

—Zechariah 14:1–5 (New Living Translation)

The coming of the Lord with a sword will be a welcome sight for all those who know and love Jesus and have been waiting for Him throughout the Tribulation. But the millions of others who opposed Jesus will tremble in fear. They will grieve. They will mourn. They will understand that this is the moment of their judgment.

Jesus will arrive with fierceness and wrath. He will defeat the Antichrist and the False Prophet, throwing them into the lake of fire. The description of this scenario in Scripture is explicit:

*Then I saw the beast and the kings of the world and their
armies gathered together to fight against the one sitting
on the horse and his army. And the beast was captured,
and with him the false prophet who did mighty miracles
on behalf of the beast—miracles that deceived all who
had accepted the mark of the beast and who worshiped his
statue. Both the beast and his false prophet were thrown
alive into the fiery lake of burning sulfur. Their entire
army was killed by the sharp sword that came from the
mouth of the one riding the white horse. And the vul-
tures all gorged themselves on the dead bodies.*

—Revelation 19:19–21 (New Living Translation)

This final event ends human history as we know it
in this age. It will be followed by the next age, which
is known as the Millennial Reign. The Bible says this
will be a period of one thousand years—that's where the
name comes from—and it represents the final one thousand years of human history on the earth.

The Millennial Reign will be very different from the
Tribulation and any of the years that came before it.

THE THOUSAND-YEAR REIGN

Sinful men have ruled the earth throughout its history.
That's why it has always been plagued with violence and
war. But when Jesus returns, He will rule the earth for
one thousand years from Jerusalem. His Church—His

followers—will rule and reign with Him during this time. Under the rule of Jesus, the earth will finally experience true peace.

If you are a new follower of Jesus, this may be the hardest part of this book to understand, but this future event will soon become a reality for you if you survive the Tribulation. Before the Rapture, the eyes of many Christians would glaze over when pastors and Bible scholars would talk about the Millennial Reign. It seems like such a long time, and until the Rapture, this period seemed so far into the future.

"What does this have to do with me?" they would ask. "What does the thousand years have to do with anything I'm going through?"

But that's because they didn't understand a very important biblical truth: *What we do now at the end of this age makes a difference in the next age.*

In Revelation chapter 2, an angel delivers important messages to several churches directly from Jesus. One of those is to the church in Thyatira. First, Jesus warns them about following false teachers. Then He encourages them to endure in their faith until the end:

> *"I will ask nothing more of you except that you hold tightly to what you have until I come. To all who are victorious, who obey me to the very end,*
>> *To them I will give authority over all the nations. They will rule the nations with an iron rod and smash them like clay pots.*

They will have the same authority I received from my Father, and I will also give them the morning star!"
—Revelation 2:24–28 (New Living Translation)

This is a major promise from Jesus, the Son of God. He's delivering this promise to the early believers in Thyatira, but He is also making a promise to those living today—even those, like you, who live in the world after the Rapture.

He is telling you to obey until the very end.

Overcome. Endure. Stand firm in your faith.

For those who held onto their faith before the Rapture, he caught them up in the air to prevent them from going through the horrors of the Tribulation. That's because the Bible says God saved us rather than pouring out His anger on us (1 Thessalonians 5:9). The Bible describes these believers as the "Bride of Christ" who will spend the seven years of the Tribulation in God's presence. When Jesus returns in the Second Coming, they will return with Him.

But some believers, like you, decided to trust Jesus after the Rapture. If you took the first part of this book seriously, you came to faith during the events of the Tribulation. What's next for you?

HOLY AUTHORITY

The Bible says all believers will rule and reign with Christ during the thousand years. That means *all* believers, including new believers during the last days. You will be given authority at the end of the Tribulation, along with all those who were martyred during the past seven years. The Book of Revelation describes this glorious moment:

> *Then I saw thrones, and the people sitting on them had been given the authority to judge. And I saw the souls of those who had been beheaded for their testimony about Jesus and for proclaiming the word of God. They had not worshiped the beast or his statue, nor accepted his mark on their foreheads or their hands. They all came to life again, and they reigned with Christ for a thousand years.*
> —Revelation 20:4 (New Living Translation)

Everyone who gave his or her life to Christ will reign with Christ. New believers who survived the Tribulation. New believers who were killed during the Tribulation. The believers who were alive at the time of the Rapture and the believers over the centuries who followed Jesus faithfully.

All of them will reign with Christ for a thousand years.

Who will they reign over? That's a good question. Before the Rapture, some Bible teachers disagreed on the interpretation of this teaching, and of course it remains hard to make accurate claims about a future event—even given the prophetic descriptions of it in the Bible. But many scholars believe that a significant number of unbelievers will survive the Tribulation. The world may be a smoldering ruin, but some individuals will somehow escape this period of warfare and judgment with their lives.

If they do, they will find themselves subject to the thousand-year rule of Jesus. It's possible that some of these unbelievers will be so wicked that God doesn't allow them to die. These will be the worst of the worst, and God will supernaturally keep them from death so they must experience the Thousand-Year Reign. They will discover firsthand what it is like to be subject to Jesus and the saints, who will rule with an "iron rod."

That phrase indicates severity. Prior to the Tribulation, the world existed in an age of grace in which God withheld his punishment for sin and rebellion. But that age will end with the Rapture and Tribulation. The world had its chance.

After the Second Coming, the age of grace will be no more. Jesus will set up His throne on earth, from Jerusalem, and share authority with His followers, the saints. We will never sin again, so there will be no need for grace. We will have the same authority that Jesus has as members of His righteous government, ruling with power and reigning over the unbelieving world for a thousand years.

The government will be perfect during the Millennium. It will be holy and just. For the Christians of the world, there could not be a better scenario. There won't be Democrats or Republicans, political parties, or religious denominations. Jesus will be the King of Kings and the Lord of Lords. We will rule with perfect truth and morality as the Word of God is exalted over all the earth.

As a new believer in Christ who obeys to the end, *you will be part of that reign.* You will be included in that rulership. What a tremendous honor it will be during the Millennium to share authority given by Jesus Christ and be able to govern according to the Word of God. It will be wonderful.

But do you think the unbelievers will like it? Of course they won't. They'll hate it! These wicked people, for the first time in their lives, will be forced to abide by God's rules. Having refused to repent and receive Christ, the Millennial reign of Jesus—the rule of a sharp sword and iron rod—will be their punishment. That's why the Bible says they eventually will rise up and try to kill the saints and Jesus at the end of the Millennium.

As the Book of Revelation describes it, the period of a thousand years begins with Satan bound in chains and thrown into a bottomless pit:

Then I saw an angel coming down from heaven with the key to the bottomless pit and a heavy chain in his hand. He seized the dragon—that old serpent, who is the devil, Satan—and bound him in chains for a thousand years. The angel threw him into the bottomless pit, which he then shut and locked so Satan could not deceive the nations anymore until the thousand years were finished.
—Revelation 20:1–3 (New Living Translation)

But after the saints rule and reign with Christ for a thousand years, Satan will be released from his prison. He will attempt to lead a rebellion against the forces of God. He will go on a rampage in his final opportunity to defeat Jesus:

> *When the thousand years come to an end, Satan will be let out of his prison. He will go out to deceive the nations—called Gog and Magog—in every corner of the earth. He will gather them together for battle—a mighty army, as numberless as sand along the seashore. And I saw them as they went up on the broad plain of the earth and surrounded God's people and the beloved city. But fire from heaven came down on the attacking armies and consumed them. Then the devil, who had deceived them, was thrown into the fiery lake of burning sulfur, joining the beast and the false prophet. There they will be tormented day and night forever and ever.*
> —Revelation 20:7–10 (New Living Translation)

Satan will arouse the nations of the earth who hate Jesus and the saints. He will lead them in battle to try to overcome the righteous. But the uprising won't be successful.

With fire and destruction, God will put down the rebellion from His throne. He will judge the dead according to their works. The old heaven and earth will pass away and in its place the Lord will create a new heaven and new earth filled with the light of Jesus.

At the end of the age, the smoldering ruin of the Tribulation will have been transformed into paradise. Not a metaphorical paradise, but a literal, physical kingdom of God where we will live forever with Jesus. The Bible describes it this way, and that description is so incredible it will serve as the end of this chapter:

> *I saw no temple in the city, for the Lord God Almighty and the Lamb are its temple. And the city has no need of sun or moon, for the glory of God illuminates the city, and the Lamb is its light. The nations will walk in its light, and the kings of the world will enter the city in all their glory. Its gates will never be closed at the end of day because there is no night there. And all the nations will bring their glory and honor into the city. Nothing evil will be allowed to enter, nor anyone who practices shameful idolatry and dishonesty—but only those whose names are written in the Lamb's Book of Life.*
>
> **—Revelation 21:22–27 (New Living Translation)**

THE END

FINAL ENCOURAGEMENT

If you have gotten this far in this little book, the most important outcome of your reading will be whether you have given your life to Jesus or not. The Rapture is now in the past and you are about to enter the worst season of world history. You may be immersed in it already.

The fact that you are alive and well enough to discover this book, read this far, and hopefully make the decision to follow Christ indicates that God indeed has a plan for you. He hasn't given up on you. If you gave your heart to Him, He welcomes you into His kingdom.

The only problem is your timing. Even though you acted in the final years of the age of grace, you waited until the door had closed with the Rapture of the Church. As a result, now you will have to experience the horrors of the reign of the Antichrist—the most evil man in world history—and the judgments of the Tribulation.

But you can endure because God is with you. Jesus promises you His strength. God will reward your perseverance if you obey until the very end.

In the days to come, as you put in the effort to read the Bible, locate other Christians, and stand firm against evil, please understand that God sees you. He knows everything you are going through. He recognizes the difficulty of the world you are living in now. He not only sees the sin and chaos, but He is *with* you amid the sin and chaos. He is protecting you and giving you strength to continue in faith.

The Bible makes this very clear, with a number of promises about persevering through trials. God will reward you when you stand for Him:

> *"But as for you, be strong and courageous, for your work will be rewarded."*
>
> **—2 Chronicles 15:7 (New Living Translation)**

Withstanding hardship earns the promise of ruling with Him, including during the coming Millennium:

> *If we endure hardship,*
> *   we will reign with him.*
> *If we deny him,*
> *   he will deny us.*
>
> **—2 Timothy 2:12 (New Living Translation)**

He promises to fulfill His purpose in you, to cover you with his steadfast love, and to never abandon you:

The LORD will work out his plans for my life—
for your faithful love, O LORD,
endures forever.

—Psalm 138:8 (New Living Translation)

He will empower you to do everything you need to stay strong:

For I can do everything through Christ, who gives me strength.

—Philippians 4:13 (New Living Translation)

He will strengthen you with His power and might:

We also pray that you will be strengthened with all his glorious power so you will have all the endurance and patience you need. May you be filled with joy, always thanking the Father. He has enabled you to share in the inheritance that belongs to his people, who live in the light.

—Colossians 1:11–12 (New Living Translation)

He will rescue you from evil and deliver you into safety:

Yes, and the Lord will deliver me from every evil attack and will bring me safely into his heavenly Kingdom. All glory to God forever and ever! Amen.

—2 Timothy 4:18 (New Living Translation)

In fact, the Apostle Paul may have even been writing about the Tribulation when he penned these words to the Church in Rome:

We can rejoice, too, when we run into problems and trials, for we know that they help us develop endurance. And endurance develops strength of character, and character strengthens our confident hope of salvation. And this hope will not lead to disappointment. For we know how dearly God loves us, because he has given us the Holy Spirit to fill our hearts with his love.

—Romans 5:3–5 (New Living Translation)

These are dark days, but the Bible makes it very clear that brighter days are coming. If you can hold on, keeping your thoughts on God and looking to the future with hope, the Holy Spirit will give you the patience and power to withstand your present circumstances.

Soon, you will live in the presence of God with a perfect body and a perfect relationship with Jesus and everyone else around you. There will be no more death, pain, or sorrow—only joy! Keep this truth in mind when you are surrounded by heartache and persecution. The current chaos is only temporary.

If you have given your life to Jesus, He promises an eternity of joy, pleasure, and happiness. He wants better for you than you even want for yourself. He wants to help you with anything and everything. He will always be with you, and He is listening to your prayers. You can ask Him for help to guide you during these dark times.

Jesus Christ loves you more than anyone has ever loved you.

You have started well, and the Lord is with you. He will always be with you. He will never leave you. He is gracious and patient and will never give up on you. On your worst day, He will be your best friend. And regardless of what is going on in the world or what evil people are doing, God is above it all. All-knowing and all-powerful, He is bigger than any problem or enemy. Depend on Him and He will be faithful to you!

God bless you.

The Tipping Point Prophecy Update

by Jimmy Evans

In this timely email newsletter, Jimmy Evans draws on decades of study, experience and biblical expertise as he explains the striking parallels between current world events and the prophecies of Scripture.

Subscribe to this newsletter for just $7/month. You'll get insightful emails every week, exclusive access to podcast episodes and much more.

ENDTIMES.COM